SENSE OF SEASON

Oxford County - Toronto - Montréal
1982 - 1987

SENSE OF SEASON

(1988)

David Manicom

(1960 -

Dominique —

Merci. J'espère que
Tu aimeras cettes poèmes

Dav.
April 90

Porcépic Books
Victoria, Canada

Published by Porcépic Books, a division of Press Porcépic Limited, 4252 Commerce Circle, Victoria, British Columbia, V8Z 4M2, Canada, with financial assistance from the Canada Council.

Canadian Cataloguing in Publication Data

Manicom, David, 1960-
    Sense of season

    Poems
    ISBN 0-88878-280-2

    I. Title.
PS8576.A54S4 1988   C811'.54   C88-091621-4

For Teresa

CONTENTS

I Unweaving

II Sense of Season

III Slow Portrait

ACKNOWLEDGEMENTS

Most of these poems were first published in the following journals, often in somewhat different versions: *Acta Victoriana, The Antigonish Review, Anthology of Magazine Verse and Yearbook of American Poetry* (U.S.A.), *Arc, The Canadian Forum, Contemporary Verse 2, Descant, Event, The Fiddlehead, Grammateion, Grain, The Malahat Review, Matrix, Poetry Montréal, Poetry Canada Review, PRISM international, Quarry Magazine, Rubicon, University of Toronto Review* and *Waves.* I would like to thank the editors, particularly Brenda Riches at *Grain* for her time and persistence.

I owe gratitude to Bill Martin of Ingersoll, Peter O'Brien and Paul Jennings for their support, and to Adrian and Lucy King-Edwards for crucial encouragement and their ability to make Montréal a community.

In a variety of cities, countries and continents, Charles Foran read all of these poems, some of them many times, and made innumerable improvements. He also suggested the basic structure of the collection. His help went far beyond all reasonable claims of friendship.

Teresa Marquis was, on all occasions, first reader and best critic.

I

UNWEAVING

"I will move my hand in the darkness like a plough,
And fall with the full heaviness of the harvest."

Mandelstam

Mute Youth

A mute youth as I gather
the quilt to my throat waits in shadow;
pale with holding his blood still, lifts a slow
hand to smoke his lungs' fire.

Evening falls from the mountain forests
and gathers in the curtain's folds.
He lingers near the mirror as I rest,
pale clear face, smoking his gold eyes,
the contempt of youth infinitely old,
waiting. I will repeat the lie

and sleep. In the morning
the girl bearing the white bowl
will stand watching the opening
of my eyes. The earth is bound by an old charm
that chains us to freedom. Thousands in the cool
of dawn are labouring on the broken hills
to lift the mist with their arms.

Paying the Rent, 1789-1861

And tore his tired tongue from the milling
of fine replies to impatient Squires
demanding the tithing of his hired thoughts.
A possible motive to fit the tale,
to reason out its humpbacked, ploughman's shape.
He jerked the next scene from the heart
of his lean, simple story; tore his bones
from his chair by the fire after work.
Heavy with the middle age and four sons
tore his paunch from the supper table
and wandered into the ocean.

Walked off that damned sailing outhouse
with dung on his elbows and wandered
through New York's Babel to the next green sea,
past the continent's navel at Niagara
where a broken shard of British gentry
sold him unseen acres fives days west.
Wore the mottled sunlight on the blazed
surveyor's line that Simcoe called a street
in Upper Canada, 1831.

Five days found him paused in seamless brush,
no trace of mapping on its edgeless soil:
Lot 23, Concession 1.
The land had never heard his name.

They told him in the village he would find
his farm this far beyond the last landmark --
but he had brought it with him.
Its graces had been more easily seen
from the open, blasted decks of Yorkshire moors.
As he stood he saw this land owned him.
The rhythm of his eyes' long fences jarred
with these milling, uncentred maples,
these straight grey lords of his caught breath.

He clenched his hands, nervous at his new youth.
He had been married to an older bride
with foreign tastes.

By the next spring when his wife walked inland
beside four sons, a fifth upon her back,
he had fitted a lobe of his brain
into the woods to make them feel at home.

The cabin grew square from the round trunks.
Year by year he found a spot to lay
most of the space he carried in his head,
jammed it into what earth and air was there,
jimmied the corners with axe and spade,
furrowed the sandy loam as straight as type,
fitted the cracks with next year's scheme.

When his jaw fell open after thirty years
black soil beneath the cornfield
crawled slowly through the box and filled his skull
with its own dark plan.

Unweaving

My father passes
on the land, over, over
the furrow's deep lines,

over the shadowed grooves
in the hill's brow, smoothing, passing.
He surrounds the sun's field
with the patience of his long day
passing from dark into dark.

The tractor rolls against fall
as he wears the ridges down,
a calm combing, a burnishing.
What the plough edge broke.

From the house, his levelling
has made us see the shape
of the perfect land for the first time,
a young god's brown skin
rising from this growing old.

He passes steadily
as his constant words over my head
on a path polished
like the doorstep into home.

For seed he would not choose
he wore me young and fertile
with all his love and aging.

Midnight, doppler

In September the weeds dry paper sharp
along Concession roads between the stalks,
the chicory curls its blue-purple tongues.

The Friday night pickups are rising whine
and falling roar that bisect fields of calm
like the birth cord cut. Rise turns to fall in
never quite and always was, a moment
lost in the folding hand, tonight's doppler
of open throttle, throat, the fanning lights
gone down the tunnel beyond the blind,
the walls, the mother's bedside reading lamp.
The hours of weekend drink their thirst,
are desperate and deaf to desperation,
immune to ambition and the quiet girl
and this poem within them. Parties in barns,
in yards as wide as the climbing fields,
the rides between, school and chores and school.
The sound they make is to hell with the dance,
and is grand and heartpounding and lonely,

is the phone jangling in the night's nerve.

Piano Lessons

In the house where my mother was born,
her mother died. Through last years she languished
in two back rooms of sprawling farmhouse,
her mind's winter cabin, the rest closed off.
Dust-tight closets and sealed hallways hung
powder grey rectangles above her head
like rows of empty tombs, like spent streets
of Dawson. On the windows plastic sheets
tattered on their rusting tacks, rags wadded
under shut doors against a cold draft.

Eight children flitted through bedrooms,
electric in the corridors of her bones,
running like gold through her blued fingers.
As a child, visiting while she lingered
near the iron stove -- rousing scarlet embers
with an ash-tipped poker -- I always laughed,
for she lingered full of *By Jimminy!* and
Great day in the morning! -- laughed, not hearing sand
sifting loose as the yellow bricks flaked
like mica, as the next spring's ivy snaked
into the new splits and fingered them
with its plying green cords. I thought then,
visiting with my mother, that the house
itself was small and close, that grandma's mouth
grew brilliant flowers all day long,
both when we came and when she sat alone.

*

In the foundation of the wind-gray barn
the awkward mortared fieldstones waited,
pink and bruised, harder than their bonds.

*

As a girl my mother received one year
of lessons, a sip each week in town --
till falling prices cropped frivolity.
Set off by Don Messer's on TV
she would finger the Black Hawk Waltz
at our piano on a Saturday night,
alone, without music, her arms light,
and we heard the graceful tides of notes
behind the noise of hockey. Yet my throat
did not catch, I was not excavated
by her dancing, girlish hands. Now, too late

I remember the old house finally empty
and wading through the wild front lawn
that only a windbrake of cedars
was keeping from the fields. The lights were gone
in the back windows. We tramped dark, fecund
galleries of rooms behind the doors
I had never seen open. On a hardwood floor
at the cluttered foot of a front staircase
stepping faintly upward into gloom
there was a piano, squatting under boxes
and a random drift of family papers.
The walnut veneer had chipped like dried
fingernails. Mother moved a dust-furred ash tray,
folded back the wooden lid, and touched
one yellowed ivory tooth. She listened, taut,
composing how the pitch was smoothed away.

Wilsons

Room knotted with blood-ties, aunts dabbing
the holy water out of their eyes,
swallowed sobs jerk from the still aisle.
Uncles watching their black shoes while the stabs
of mourning circle their weak spaces,
nervous with guarded guts, set faces.

Curtain drawn, the father and mother
pass behind for the closing of the lid.
A strangled sound reaches us, another,

the uncles move their haunches, breathe,
we pray *No more*, brace, the noises
lurch into us again, loose a trapped spasm
as wild as raw surf at night.

*

After we carried the shimmering box
(shaken that there was weight, that our arms
would have to heft against
what was inside), on the farm
beside the field of stones a ploughman,
seeing the string of inching cars,
stopped his tractor in the midst of turning sod down
so that with only the accurate silence
would we put her into the ground.

Oxygen

First blackbird lights the spine
of a tree swamp-rotted,
shaven, branches age-lopped:
at the knobs the resin

dries, a thin amber scab.
Mist totem, ankles chill
in grey March vigil.
Blackbird with red shoulder badge

scratches the slate sky
with his metal whistle
and flees, pumping the flags
of his arms, the only

colour in the world.
I stand in my footsteps.
The tree, marooned in quag
without hands, forgets to fall.

North over blunt dun stubble
of summer's blonde rye,
wings, like pulsed clean blood,
welding my eye.

Autumn Child

The velvet scalp of an infant
heart breathing through the membrane
of the crown's bruise. Inside your cry
the shadowed gums' slick pink line.

Arm-mangered, your father's stride
back the lane through fall's elegy
of rusted ochre, saps burnt and dried.
Fence-row's brittle energy

smokes under snap of metal sky.
Against his flannel, October
chill cannot reach you, ecstasy
of newness, delicate tinder.

Yellow-rocket gold as old sun,
maples caught in the forge of evening.
Your father quiet, bearing you home,
plundered by understanding.

After Our Children Had Gone to School

Behind the cattle-warm barn
the gnarled crab-apple carried all winter a burden
of sagging shoulders by the pond's dull skin,
hung twisted knuckles down like claws.

Winds warm and light as a swallow's voyage
lifted one year the layers of lace shawls one by one
from the black-bundled widows in corner pews,
candles blessed the damp lines of their faces
into rivers of light and this pain

trickles down cut ridges to the pond in April,
skateslashes dissolve, the ice in slow retreat from shore
to a glass-edged island drowning in sun,
and free water in this silver ring surrounding
the cows' steaming muzzles in the first afternoon outdoors.

Pockmarks by the pools, the oozing suck of hoofs,
the pasture laced with green by voices. On the boughs
so many blossoms the orioles sang onward into the evening.

Then thrown on the water by the bentfingered tree
so many blossoms pink as roseshadow,
white as the wedding in an old woman's future.

Walked down in that time after breakfast
alone after our children had gone to school.
When I came to the spring so unaccountably many blossoms
that I believed forever you had come there in the night
and stood by the stars dreaming of my impossible love for you.

Stillbirth

I have lived so long in the breech of the womb,
pulled the green from the head of day to find the core,
what I came for. The sun grew full with summer

but gave birth to slow loss, just the falling leaves
like calendar months, and a pale, tasteless heart
swept into another trash of spines and peelings.

The hour decomposes its intricate fruit,
I'll burn tomorrow too. I remember
tucking each night gently behind your curving ear

in the time we spent reading eyes like cups of tea,
learning each speck of leaf, each subtle flinch of pain,
preparing for today, breakfasts on the terrace.

I haven't seen you for a long time. You send cards.

The cow's black and white barrel sides heaved like quick fear.
My father wrapped a thick rope on the knobbed, blind hooves
of the calf, emerging like stumps from the underground,

and pulled. I pulled. He knew it was already dead
as it slid, fell a long smooth slap onto straw.
The mother turned her soft dark head from far away,

some long ago, looked, and did not lick her wound.
It lay on its side, a pink string from the belly.
When I think of you I think of my father

and his red hands, and how Hawley's Stock Removal
sent a thin man who took the rope that father left
and dragged the calf up the gravel driveway to his truck.

The head bumped gently as the pebbles rolled.

Textured

The geese free their great silent bodies
from the slate wall of cloud with white throats,
a frieze of sound leaning upon air
as the feet reach for the silver film.
I have fallen from this autumn sleep
against the finely cutting wedge
of a siren's distant, drowned lament.

The nights come in like sinking stones
on October winds that teach our hands
their cold skin sacks are filled with bones.
Again and again a still slow motion
beauty shows to us its passing
high on the fading pageant of the sky;
or once, or twice, stoops as a wild
down-fingered god to our stillest water.
They are silent, fluid as my childhood
until the white throats call for lead
with texture for the grey, dumb world.
And you rise in my throat of dreams
to careen the city streets of our lost night.
This is what I wanted to remember.

La Potterie, fermé

Bee hum   heavy bodies rebound gently
against air   hang in the faces of mallow
dust-purple pale with heat   or orange lilies
long-tongued with the heat   curved as swallows
while the trees lean slightly to all sky

and the sky slides heavily toward the edge
of this green table where we gather   hungry
for air   heavy and throbbed   August tea
afternoon   wind resting under the hedges
leaving slow whine in the ear   the bees

bobbing in fluid doze   the preservation
of our slowness   barkless limbs climbing to death
from a live root   in the porch corner
old broom with blunt straws leaning without breath
against the clapboards   the lake blue cold

and very far away.   I am waiting
for the children to come home some day.
The basement is filled with unfired clay.

                    North Hatley, Québec

Haying

The crouched baler creeps along hay-row
bound on inward spiral to the field's crown,
dragging the baled residue, track's ripeness
knotted, stacked, creaking on wagon boards.

Crawls, arm thrashing, compacting, thudded roar
at the present core of slow procession,
eats the tangled hair of raked hay.
Slender sway of green meadow hacked, flayed;
a scythe our breathing swings. Catching our eye
the small terror of quick field mice
darting into their bald sky.

At the conclusion
of slow-narrowing perimeters, the fusion
of barren field and full wagons,
of late supper and our sunburn and dust.
At sunset the stretched membrane bright,
allowing into our gathering space
not enough, light.

Anchor Post

I drove from downtown for one last traipse
down a sidewalk sunk into lawn, its line
of cement islands, back a chicory-blue lane
to turn on a hill and watch the barns stand,

abandoned ships. August twitch-grass rasping
at my thighs, steady *sip sip* of crickets.
The fence posts were leaning. Keeping them straight
had helped keep father standing, balanced

against need, thwarting the earth from tugging
their wood back into humus, the mossed lawns
from creeping over the nicks of his spade,
the hedgerows from colonizing fields.

Even one corner-post, waist thick but gnawed
near soil, had begun to pitch down its head.
(Half a day we'd have spent sinking that shaft
of white, shaven trunk into a four foot hole,

tamping the loose dirt with an iron pole,
bracing this anchor on its slender neighbour
with looped wire racheted to a tight steel braid
by a shovel's work-polished handle.)

Now the grey wood is rivered by wind,
the grain engraved, and knots where branches
once veered toward light have fallen away
until the dried post is filling with eyes.

Its rotting top has sunk into a nest
for finches and a portal for rain,
so decay can attack as it attacks
these counties, from inside out, eating toward skin.

There is no taut fence for it to anchor now;
the loss of what it once held up helps pull
it down. Only a few strings rusted to black
cling between the tilted posts beneath the grass,

slack and gripless under whispering grass
until, perhaps, near the end of October
when the anchor is gone and the other posts
have been hauled and split and stacked in cords,

an employee of the corporate farm
that will buy and manage this stead, this small
nest-egg of acres, might feel a snag
in his six-furrow plough when levelling the land

into one, long, uninterrupted field,
and climb down to untangle the sock
from a bit of black web.
I could see father, holding the U-shaped

staples in his teeth as his smooth hammer
clipped the strands snug . . . . I clamped both hands
to the sunken top for leverage and jumped up
to give my weight. Stubborn fibres creaked

and split as I hugged and wrestled it flat.
It lay, thick as a barrel. I sat, then lashed
with my fist, skinning one knuckle red,
cursed its ridiculous, graceless shape,

pounded dull thuds on its passive, weathered shell.
He'd balanced so long, on the thin borders
between drench and drought, harvest and bankruptcy,
working repairs in the narrow regions of air

next to the spinning knives of machinery,
taking the edges into his creasing life.
He'd balanced so long. Now he's fallen over
and these fences are following him down.

The Country West of Toronto

Travelling single file,
insect-limbed colossi
of Ontario Hydro
in spaced processional,
city bound pilgrims
gawk-legged in the townships.

Strung to the soothed rivers,
dip of frost-coloured thread
across sky, a deep hum
in rain, strobe thundercracks
muffled to equation,
doled, played along the wires.
Splay-footed on hills
they turn ploughs from their paths,
furrows loop like water
flowing pattern around stones --
the shape of eyes and rain.
Blades working back, curving back
pass by pass toward the
straight, the orginal
line of striking out
from the field's raw border,
sight ruled on a far tree.

Striding through October mist
stripped skyscrapers
transporting the river's kick.
Southern Ontario
farmland, highway-veined,
a region near two desires,
awkward homeland wedged
between the named cities
and the country as it holds
in the sweet mind.

Looking Across

The house hollow now behind him,
chair drawn up, his silent white head.
Poplar leaves cool to pale green in autumn.
Between his morning gaze and vision
they hang, framed by aching stillness
among the blood and fire of maples.
Water.
As motionless as memories
of oval faces in worn photographs.

Growing translucent, exposing skeletons.
And the sun through them.

Accumulation of air, the diluted sky.
Paling. The space between,
intervals of the heart muscle.
Breakfast, lunch, dinner at evening.

Then the slow lisps of the wind
moving his eyes. He can no longer
interrupt the light, his lids thin scales
etched with veins. The pebbled drive,
the lawn, its clipped hedges,
do not betray him, do not change
into any other world.
They merely begin to whisper.

Winter is white.

Through the last summer they had to tape
her splitting skin, her bones were wrapped
in crackling tissue paper
like the hour's gift.

When he looks out
the leaves hang very still.
Then they are on the ground.

The window is suddenly full
of the other side of the street.

II

SENSE OF SEASON

"The voyagers we cannot follow
Are the most haunting."

John Montague

Sense of Season

1

You know from a black page the winter's tale
  of stiff faces grown yellow. Uncharmed, smoke
    curls from your nostril to the iron stove:
  you sensed a grandmother's hard arms, awoke
burning maple, grandfather's white shock. You fail

to find your mother as she moves
  about the long table, a slender girl, smell
    of lilacs sculpting the faint air. This scene
  of the burning, yellowing photograph tells
you silently the womb has been removed

through which the grandparents might reach, demeans
  that which they meant in their summer season
    of the green scent of dry hay, the hard stalk.
  The stones are falling. Your tropes cannot reason
with such old children as evening leans

the overalled uncles on their elbows. They talk
  of what the stolid radio had said
    before it fell silent in a fall forgotten
  with the acrid smell of Europe's dead
from the crossed wires. Among their leaves you walk

but find no page in the drawer's false bottom
  to remember the years' dismemberment.
    She is not there; the child will not contain you.
  You cannot regale what the wind has bled, scent
from the yellow piles, the rusted face of autumn.

2

You said you loved her -- and left her, closing the door
   of her next moment with the softest click.
      Then came back to visit, to make the dead feel dead,
   and learned how it was. It was not the trick
you had done with mirrors, in the spring, before,

tilting reflections until what was said
   had not been said, and black pools did not contain
      in their murmuring films the forked shadows of self.
   When you went back in June her room was the same
regardless of angles. You were somehow misled

by the civilized chink of cups, the drugged, bright health
   of violet eyes shadowed by the rinds of nights
      they had watched through. You called her "Dear."
   You sat in the past without future, polite
sips like drowning breaths, speeches moving with stealth

through the minefields of contradiction. The clear
   cry of the passing summer, last smoke rising
      from the dead child's mouth, the home village strafed.
   You have cast the now from the safe abiding
echoes of then, slid from new matrix into here.

Place your mother poised at the piano on the graph
   of what you are now not. You came back to absence
      thinking suffering was only something silent
   and hard. Your love was polite, her pain so intense
its only sound was a shamed, nervous laugh.

3

As though walking through the silent summer dawns
      without having slept, dark drowsing trees
            still, brooding, new against the light of pale sky,
      without the flow of dissolving night to free
the estranged mind from this familiar lawn.

The folded blades tracing strands of a yesterday
      strung to clotted roots by the sun's liturgy.
            Birth without death: a twin grows in the heart's interval,
      colour climbs from stem to autumn's revelry
cell by cell. You start: the mirror's mimesis decays.

Suddenly your father has grown old, eyes small
      when he comes in, cold from the increasing labour
            of ploughing the corduroy hills for spring
      before the snow has fallen. The dark savour
of soil haunts his constant, quiet denial.

The child mother a stranger, love a fathoming
      of death by inconsistency. You can see
            in the glass your father about your eyes,
      a line of jaw growing intimately
into his dark plot, the angels faintly wailing.

A verged limb of new vision, you see the cries
      of all branching foilage. Seated on the monument
            to soldiers changed by death of change, in ice-clear air
      an old woman collects dawn's throbbing nourishment
from the wings she feeds her bread of eulogy.

4

Water falls from the fountain and returns:
   momentary drape on the veined form of air.
      The eye engraved by shape, the flowing gesture lost,
   her hair brushed gently into a dark year.
A log in this forest, you see the totems burn

and swing across the sky to leaves and dust.
   Each charred, phoenix face resumes an attitude.
      In autumn you were climbing the blade of rock
   as you had for years, tasting the small fruits,
the berries under leaves, the wood's slow rust --

when the summit was. The frozen wave of rock
   rolled. Small pebbles clattered from the page's edge
      into the inarticulate pale. Your fear,
   the undreamable nightmare, whispered that the judge
of that place gives back no echo. You walk

slowly back into yourself, tongue on the clear
   gust of spring breeze that unfolds reseeded time
      and folds you into a new place. You awoke,
   belly green with moss, lost in the decayed design,
centre hollow, damp, turned to pulp with the year,

empty from sky's deep lungs, a space for the wind's work.
   They say that you fell embracing your shadow.
      In any event it is gone. And there
   on the brink it was a flavour so new
on your new lips that summer yawned and blue spoke.

5

Lifting the lens cap's slow lid, peel the bed's
   woolen horizons. All of it touches you.
      On one arm as the clock radio declares
   from crossed wires that no time has passed or been passed through,
that in the South Atlantic sons are dead.

Your infant daughter has fine strands of spring hair.
   She walks from your hand with teeter-totter steps,
      warming her doll legs for forest paths. Cyclists
   purr by on stable circles. The park sleeps.
Seasons do not change the fact that she starts there

with you already here. Time spins, lists
   drunkenly, unknown faces in the bathroom glass;
      but proportion goes untouched. You are bound
   this time's space from her, mute strangers cast
on separate strands of river shore in gathering mist.

And her grandmother a photograph found
   on a black page. Toward the violet's eye
      a flush of deeper purple. Snow falls through the lights
   into dark hair, fills the tree's elbow. A drunk dies
beneath yesterday's news. Only silence resounds.

You want a line in the tale of the summer night
   where the stranger's head is fiction, where the green
      tracing giant turns in the bed, murmurs, reaches:
   reaches like lilac to the other sleeper's dream
a touch beyond auroral typeless white.

III

SLOW PORTRAIT

". . . where there had been
just a makeshift hut to receive the music."

Rilke

A Change of States

The mountain fills night's door
like a stranger.

Your voices awake new colours
between the words my eyes have known.

I have seen a small village
with a wall against the sea
where a woman with carved palms
handles her foreign fruit
like your round, citrous speech.

The shadow in Montréal
in the alley we see
from our wedding bed at night,
has a darker tone.

Ombre. Sleeping,
your hair falls halfway
across your crescent face.
A tide hauls silence.

The sparrows chase each other in rings
among the leaves in Carré-Saint-Louis,
smooth untangling arcs of wind.

To this city I have brought
a barbarous tongue,
a store of scalpels
in a drunken hand.

Each dawn I find your body beside me
unfolding the light like a new page
of our *dictionnaire.*

Househusband, 5:30 p.m.

The stained, sticking dishes rise
like a totem to ambition in decline.
A bit of ketchup, a piece of wing,
a crumb the wind flicked from my page.
When you come home swinging the day
over your shoulder, sealed at five
in that tidy, compartmented purse,
bearing cheques blessed with signatures,
I am cleaving the flesh for supper
at the cutting board, and prying
language with my teeth
to give you all the bitter words
that today you seem to deserve
for never once deserving them.

Even this is an ugly offering.

Overcome with love's clumsiness
the knife cuts apart while I gather sums
of each day's unwritten words
to salt the wounds I open with the wine.
The odd finger finds its way into the stew,
I flavour all with pepper, cloves, despair.
Night is falling, it is all I have prepared.
This is my body.

Some Days Near Mount Royal

Dawn got darkness up and clean for work.
Speckled the drowsing trees with wheat-straw sun.
Flung rose water from slender fingertips.
She found us later in our basement flat,
began to dry the wash on backs of chairs.
We awoke facing the same direction
like dim spoons, lay nested like vertebrae,
linked but separate, white and winged and hollowed.

Even doing dishes for two
it cannot always be ignored
that the streets of this city are steep,
that the rows of wrought-iron walkups
are stone so they will not lean, and ornate
so the reason for hardness is forgotten.
In winter the mountain white with dark etchings
from the limbs that cling along its sides;
in winter mute. The climbers descend
without the answers to anything.
On some days when the child cries, and words
line up stupidly like soldiers
and the last verse is broken by supper,
all streets run upward to that pale brow.

Some days we are so much in love
that the radio is silenced
for making our room too crowded.

Some days the time's smooth sides are pierced;
desire to be climbing crowds together
with dark fatigue in the legs.
I lie with my back to your back
far into the night.

Slow Portrait

There is a small hollow below your throat
as smooth as shadow, slack between cords,
like the palm print of a god. Breathe, wait.
I touch you there for the first time, lord
quietly here and servant, after these years
I touch you there.

I am light in this long and lengthening career,
the slow task of taking your virginity.

A full moon threads into the still street
outside our bed. You are carved in liquid.
The sun burns the shadows from leaves,
stars cannot show their green whispers,
but moonlight weaves, and the maples
                                            are laquered.
In the street green rests on the dark leaves
almost not there like
                        my marks on your thighs,
like your breathing when I'm this deep in night.

I will gather the fine shades of your virginity.
Do not move   do not move   do not
move.

Montréal Blue

In laden February, on rue St. Jacques

we are dreaming the breeding of lilacs
and shuffling on ice toward Notre Dame.
Suddenly the cold bright square
the two arms of her towers and the walk
into the blue sunrise of her altar.

Mediterranean beatitude
against our river's shell; flame's still, blue root.
The summer tourists absent,
her space empty with God, we feel crude
in our bodies, clothed in our weak intent,

here only to rest in her easy shadows
the blue of tree limbs cast on snow,
of veins cradling a breast --
not to be broken. We intimately know,
scattered in pews, our curse of changelessness.

Even Israel's angry prophets
are museful underneath the patterned stars
of her indigo firmament,
bearing the gyre of upward twisting pulpit
on their old backs. Have we too been sent?

We are in Notre Dame, our commission fades.
Bronze St. Peter dozes in a corner
with his lip-polished toe,
a girl with a hair brush, close to her work,
repaints a moment of the whole.

We are in Notre Dame. Always her blue dawn
is blooming behind the Last Supper
as we grow human and go,
never the saviours of anyone,
bearing only more sky, more hollow.

Not, as we pull the carved oaks of the doors,
reborn; but blue-washed, tropic, traced with womb.
With room to have found
and taken in one winter vision more,

the white clouds sleeping on the ground.

Pearl

A man curls under newsprint
on the hard ribs of a park bench
too narrow for his knees to warm his chest.

The moon is dreaming in the river.

He is embracing a shape of air
that fits his arms perfectly.
The bench is the day's monument.
The autumn dew does not nourish him,
it dresses the grass of the field
in strings of jewels.

The moon is dreaming in the river.

He wears someone's tweed jacket,
lectures the trees and those edging past
a stream of cries from dreams
not fitting into sunlight.
His terrible words are not tied down.

We gather a camp fire, stars climb lower.
The moon is dreaming in the river.

She has no teeth and a large coat
to keep the world in. She is
behind all of us in supermarkets
buying three-day bread and counting dimes
over and over   and we are afraid

to touch the water.

In a Station of the Montréal Metro

Under the cool earth of May
in the Metro's tiled glare
a retarded, crippled man
sends the crazy echo
of his writhing accordian
into the ears of strangers
the subway lines bring.

He fingers the struggle
with stubby hands,
his disconnected mouth
works a solo from another song.
He plays his jaunt, his tip-tap
his polka with the solemn haunt
of incomprehension in saucer eyes.
He sows the air with a paradox
that flusters your love.

His guardian's wooden wedge
locks one wheel of his chair.
A slender silver chain
twins him with his begging tin.

When the strangled beast in his lap
collapses into silence
the hovering white-haired woman
flicks swift pages on his music stand,
the long strings of black birds
flock down into his hands
and a tune plays with his arms.

Walking upstairs and into the park
the thin static of rain
is knocking petals from the boughs,
and his beer hall music beats in you,
all the nightmares you'll ever have to sing.

The Children's Crusade

We flowed in great waves with the wind and sand east from Amara
We flowed against the heretic Khomeini, rolled against his guns
Rolled row after row, a ribcage crawling on desert
Our unity was the heart, we watered the desert
Small bullets of relentless sand sang on our helmets
And I felt I had died many deaths, was marching forever
The small teeth of sand were eating our faces
The hills slewed like water under the treads of our tanks
Motes in our eyes, specks clogging the pulse of our lead
We flowed out into sun: a polished shield on each dune

We broke them, began to roll past lines of untidy bundles
Many bundles were not khaki, we did not pause to strip them
Bundles lay in ranks as if for night prayer, heads pointing west
I could not count the hundreds, the sand burned after dark

We rolled toward sacred Tigris, we rolled in evening on the world
We rolled through the evening on the vast dun world
We came on a group that surrendered while still alive
We came on a group that huddled in the trace of a river
We could see their headclothes jerking like flags in the wind
A group without uniforms, not soldiers but symbols
They were pebbles flung at our nation's stone wall

We drew near, we saw they were boys -- twelve, ten, nine years
They were more confused than afraid, furtive smiles, nervous feet
They were holding their toy guns, not thinking to lay them down
I remember their teeth and eyes, the pearls in dusk faces

We drew near   The madman sends children to his jihad
They huddled in a knot like cattle in a storm
We shot them   We moved on   Such war is men's work

The Governments Debate the Sending of Food
to the Starving Millions of Marxist Ethiopia

Here, thin grey trees gather in mist again
on hillsides of pale November under still threads of rain.
Large eyes, colour washed:
they cower with narrow limbs eaten by oxygen,
like waiting crowds in spared photos of the Holocaust.

It is November, and we are weary
of the year's unravellings that famish hope,
starvation's slow diplomacy.

This is how we feel, this voice the season:
that everywhere strange bureaucrats with careful reasons
ascend to open unopened cairns
mute since goddesses on holy mountains
and announce with exquisite clarity mere human bones.

autumn 1984

PORTRAITS: FIVE REFLECTIONS

1   Monet's Lilies of Giverny

Floating, saucers of colour
centred in the frame's waterjar.
Below, trembling eels of light;
above, the shadows of air.

Somewhere near, an old man and canvas
in streaming sun, the air
a blind, trembling artist
holding onto light, its perfect colour.

*Tonight these glass shards, wafers of light
riding water, the breathing night.*
Lilies on clear skin, hammer of sun
on bodies, their visible emanations.

Wrist contorting water to dance.
Saucers in the centre like green eyes.
Air taking from the water what it gave.
Suns, unseen, in the centre like eyes.

*Paris moons broken in the river,
chance light off your eyes I caught, lost.
The bridge lifts me like a deep breath
over the Seine, its bright coins, slipping past.*

Monet staring at his canvas after dark.

2   Water and Light

Phyllis Webb reads.
Face pale, curved nostrils,
attitude of sparrow.

Slender left wrist
lifted, persuading,
appealing to the unicorns
that almost agree to be seen.
Her voice careful, pushing the words
step by step across the swinging bridges.

She pauses, the air subsides.
She lifts a clear glass to drink,
transparent water tilts
a diminishing crystal angle.
You see a glimmer of light,
but, really, what is there
to look into?   You cannot stop
seeing through.

She pours the shivering invisible
back into her throat.
And begins again.

3   Lunacy

Li Po, 701-62

Pale moon plump as the god's eye
in my still black pasture pond
you pull at my blood's tide, my pale plump lust.

Too old, splintered and sharp
as dry bamboo, I've lost the delicate dream
that I am a butterfly dreaming.

Every morning, my mouth dry
with the sediment of wine and poems, I find
strange planets in my shimmering tea.

Yet moon, I feel the filaments
of worm-spun, clinging cocoon
as I watch my lidless lethargy of watching.

You're the same each time I blink
drunken moon-in-my-lake!
hard and round in the water-mirror's vision.

But as nights pass, and the sun chants,
desire fades. My knot unties.
Plucked organ, you grow narrow,

serpent eaten circle, you wink into darkness.
To pull your waning face to my beautiful arms
is still beyond my strength

you sly, mimicking bugger.
(The two mirrored wings of a butterfly:
an old man singing at water.)

4   Facing Switzerland

In the last photograph, James Joyce
watches his grandson Stephen teach
an unidentified dog to dance

No, don't speak, we can't hear you.
A new war muddying water,
your daughter lost, somehow mislaid;
stuck in Switzerland, left to listen
to distant annunciations,
anonymous squadrons of angels
reporting immaculate deaths,
random, without sin. It dwarfed
your sense of obscure design. Depressed,
you felt like a tidy package
as the flash bolted, the dog barked.
In the end, the family garden
hedged by Alps, a barking dog.

For the first time since words began
you felt like a tidy package,
far from your cackling voices,
supposed that was how it narrowed down
as the great whittler finished up.

Dog. Garden. Stephen. Sun.
By now, you saw, their final names
hung on them like blinding mirrors,
and with light so queerly altered
you no longer made up your mind
as you went along. You sat
slouched for photos in a yard chair,
pretending to gaze off-stage,
bony thighs crossed, dolorous, studied.

The world dies slowly around you
and leaves you alone, Switerzland,
you grumped, hedged by picket Alps,
with petulant Nora and the boy
(odious little German! fraud!)
the earth crumpled like paper,
while your muse stewed hopelessly
on your own daughter (*"Lucia"?*)
who never understood your pleas,
babbling like Anna Livia
her own language in a French asylum,
exile perfected at last.

The horizon these stone watchmen
standing up from time to time
and moving a little closer in;
oblong sentries, druidic rings
beyond the corners of dim eyes.

In Switzerland, no rhododendrons.
Walks through narrow meadows,
mountain streams cold to the lake
like your small tales for Stephen
that could never reach the sea,
thinking *Lucia, speak simply, the books*
are done, just tell poppa what you need.
It's the last country you'll come to.
The world dies slowly around you
and leaves you alone. Europe dreams

her nightmare, you find yourself
in a Swiss garden, awake again
in the middle of the night.

5   December, evening, Montréal

Look, dusk creeps from the ground. It's just four
yet the trace of snow dust is dark as gunpowder
between the stems, along the walks, an undercoat
of grey as if sky showed through the skin.

Spellbound in this lighted tower looking out,
I see myself slowly appear, looking in,
rinsed in glass, a developing photograph
of the future. The street lamps are self-enclosed
in the half light, unradiant lemon jars,
completed eyes. The offices have emptied,

I sit here high in darkening air, exiled
inside a dream, staring into warm rooms.
The grey sky lays down a hundred thin veils,
my image grows clearer and clearer and still.
Who will move first? Someday it's bound to happen.

Passing By

Afterward, there is a house to be free from.

When you are burned narrow as a pupil in sun --
out into the bush at evening, December
dwindling, the trees creaking near the river
like old mansions as the cold dries them.

Later, walking deeper, air razor-thin,
still as bone near the snow-quilted banks.
The winter water free in mid-stream,
a shining ebony snake dragging its gleam
through the narrowed aperature of ice.

In the woods the shadows and their white poplars
root from each other in seamless mirrors.

But you have not pulled loose. You carry rooms
and the other is with you, a latent mime
standing behind your head with insistent regret.
You never quite see him. The clouding sky lets
down the first flakes, they linger through slow air,
drift, down, tiny broken doves, the water
rolls its dark film onward, it is time
to pass by and the snow seems very white
as it touches the river like stars going out.

Signs of Evening

for B.D.

Colour runs from the tipped bowl.
The birch are black,
all silver drained
below earth to water
that dilutes tones of memory
with the solvent of passing.
The March sky is grey.
This is what I know
as the smoke from the houses
rises like twisted ghosts
around etched fingers and limbs,
losing itself in the grey socket
of consumptive sky --
for smoke is always greyness.
And this metaphor a habit
of the smoke-grey sky
that has no colour of its own
and finds itself at last
articulate, signified.

The rain has made my hair cold.
You have been gone
have been going
such a very long time.
It is the sky that is lost,
dissolved in the name
that belongs to slow forgetting.
The trees wait to be taken.

Burials

The faces of those who drown
beneath the surface of thought,
of eternal this, gone down.
The reflective rim that turns
an unbreachable pale stare,
tethered at the radius
of flung imagination,
the smooth and barren border
where we arrive at failure.

The faces of those who drown
beneath the surface of season,
harvested by gravity
like the blue air's sediment.
The dissolving expressions
beneath our boards of hoarding,
under the yellow leaf piles
in the days of long walking
through the cold smell of apples.

The faces of those who drown
beneath the tight skin of water.
In slow continual falling
I am a bather moving out
in a photograph's silver,
feet lost below rising sheen,
cut off cleanly at the waist
by the perfect, conquering
mirror of my advancement.

Sunset North of Sudbury

The land's old shoulders
purple in this last passion,
a breath held rock-still
in the lake basin of the lungs.
Blackness rises from the hollows
where the heavy lids of pine boughs
have held it through these afternoons.

The waves of hills
from here to Hudson Bay
break against the sky
like great stone days.
Only the strands of unmeeting rails
cut against the pattern
in long, empty lines,
a history of loneliness.

The rock faces rust in rain.
Flesh is slowly given to air.

Night rises from the roots
and falls from the world's blue flower.

Beehive Huts

Dingle Peninsula, West of Ireland

You find them, the stone cones of the hermits,
a rough pottery of the rock-sown earth,
castings of the endless serpent Patrick drove
from the soil into the mind's nest of crosses.
His path from Rome swallowed itself behind him.

The road, slow with bikes and Peugeots, runs west
between the chanting surf and the scoured hills,
mist erases the verge of sea and sky.
You find them, suddenly, twelve centuries queer,
cold and whispering, making slow peace with the land,

curving day like Kerry's black mountains.
The gnat-bitten bodies of madmen
do not lie inside, you will not stumble on saints
who can steal the world away from your hands.
The floor is smooth with your own barrenness.

These stones, perfect for fences, are not taken,
storms have not removed one from another.
Muscles cramped, here, on the dust where your foot
is. You fear to think yet thirst to believe
that myth is this small dome, where men sat

and stared at crucifixion year after year
until seagulls became pieces of wind
and eyes, sea, sky blurred into one blue mist.
You are relieved that their yellow bones,
cracked on the edges of seasons, are never found.

Gaspé, evening

in Micmac, Gaspeg, "the end of the world"

This is the sea, alone, gnawing shale
stacked by the centuries. Layers split,
somersault into space, crash like doors,
notes that compose our wordless history.
Waves hammer, water hurls from a deep gale,
drives slow lines across face, edge, shore.

Whitecaps far to sea peak, curl upward, lift,
become seagulls crying like the salt's nail
raking the crazed, striated shale of cliffs
spiked with black pine.

A trembling wire: an ocean horizon.
Black cormorant slings past with kinked neck.
Light stumbles. The ferocious loneliness
of ghostly night-borne gulls as the sun
ignites the west.

How long from this ledge to the gulf's foil,
from this beak of land, the easy slip
into the garnet belly of North Atlantic?
The membrane boils, heals.

This is the end of the world, Gaspeg,
continent's shoulder stiff with winter.
Hours below, the slow scrawl of ocean wears
into the still hub of my emptiest heart.
The pivot, the lip, the Micmac's edge --

so large I can understand losing you.
Stay at the rock's crest. This is the end
of the world, this is the seed's recoil.
Place your feet, raise your arms, play the wind,
do not step off, ever. Wait. All you can own
is praise. On the slowly bruising beach
there is agate dreaming in gravel.
We are always the edge of the world.

NOTES TO THE POEMS:

"Paying the Rent, 1789-1861": My maternal great-great-great grand--father, Richard Wilson, emigrated in 1831, followed by his wife Sarah Foster Wilson (1787-1859) in 1832.

"Wilsons": I.M. Brenda Bidwell, 1964-1982.

"Monet's Lilies of Giverny": Monet's massive, shimmering depictions of his water-lily-filled pond preoccupied him for the last ten years of his life.

"Water and Light": The poem alludes to Canadian poet Phyllis Webb's piece, "The Last Days of the Unicorn," in the *Wilson's Bowl* volume.

"Lunacy": The Chinese poet Li Po reputedly drowned attempting to kiss the reflection of the moon in a pond. The Taoist sage Chuang Tzu told of his dream that he was a butterfly. Upon waking he professed to be uncertain whether or not he was now a butterfly dreaming it was a man.

"Facing Switzerland": I am indebted for details to Richard Ellman's biography of Joyce. The words I put into Joyce's mouth are fictional.

Sense of Season

Edited by Brenda M. Sully and Eizabeth Parkinson.
Cover photograph by Sandy Reber.
Cover design by Barbara Munzar of PMB Graphics, Victoria, B.C.
This book was designed and typeset electronically by Gerry Truscott, using Aldus PageMaker ® 3.0 on an Olivetti M280 computer, and output on a QMS PS 800+ laser printer.
Typeset in Palatino, 10/12.
Printed in Canada by Hignell Printing, Winnipeg, Manitoba.

Also in Porcépic Books' *NEW POETS SERIES*:

Killing the Swan by Mark Anthony Jarman
(with photographs by Sandy Reber)
ISBN 0-88878-253-5

Showcase Animals by Linda Wikene Johnson
ISBN 0-88878-251-9

For information about these or other books published by Porcépic Books, please contact us at 4252 Commerce Circle, Victoria, British Columbia, Canada, V8Z 4M2.